S0-CBU-148

"In this publication Merrell-Ann Phare makes an important contribution to the discussion of Aboriginal rights.... Society ignores this issue and the arguments in this book at its peril."
— Justice Murray Sinclair, Chairperson, Truth and Reconciliation Commission of Canada

"Water is critical to the lives of all Canadians, and First Nations are no different. Yet, for too long we have been excluded from important discussions about the future of water in Canada and have been denied access to basic water security. We must protect water, and the ecosystems and peoples that depend upon it; First Nations, relying upon our water rights, should be front and centre in leading this charge. *Denying the Source* is an important and timely book urging us to begin this discussion ... and we must, now."
— Phil Fontaine, former National Chief, Assembly of First Nations

"This book clearly elucidates the crucial importance of indigenous peoples' effective participation in decision-making processes, especially in matters related to the ownership, control and use of water found in their territories. The denial of indigenous peoples' inherent water rights since colonization up to the present, as this book illustrates in the Canadian context, is a common experience of most indigenous peoples in various parts of the world. Merrell-Ann Phare documents how the water rights of First Nations are being violated and provides good examples of successful negotiations on water issues between indigenous peoples in Canada and the US and the respective governments which other indigenous peoples can learn from."
— Victoria Tauli-Corpuz, (Kankana-ey Igorot, Philippines), Chair, UN Permanent Forum on Indigenous Issues

DENYING THE
SOURCE

The Crisis of First Nations Water Rights

Merrell-Ann S. Phare

RMB
Victoria Vancouver Calgary

Rocky Mountain Books	Rocky Mountain Books
#108 – 17665 66A Avenue	PO Box 468
Surrey, BC V3S 2A7	Custer, WA
www.rmbooks.com	98240-0468

Library and Archives Canada Cataloguing in Publication

Phare, Merrell-Ann, 1965–
    Denying the source : the crisis of First Nations water rights / Merrell-Ann Phare.

ISBN 978-1-897522-61-5

    1. Native peoples—Legal status, laws, etc.—Canada. 2. Native peoples—Land tenure—Canada. 3. Native peoples—Canada—Government relations. 4. Water rights—Canada. 5. Water-supply—Canada. I. Title.

KE7722.N37P43 2009   346.7104'3208997   C2009-903726-2   KF8210.N37P43 2009

Printed and bound in Canada

Rocky Mountain Books gratefully acknowledges the financial support of the Government of Canada through the Book Publishing Industry Development Program (BPIDP); the Canada Council for the Arts; and the province of British Columbia through the British Columbia Arts Council and the Book Publishing Tax Credit for our publishing activities.

BRITISH COLUMBIA ARTS COUNCIL

Canada Council for the Arts   Conseil des Arts du Canada

The interior pages of this book have been produced on 100% post-consumer recycled paper, processed chlorine free and printed with vegetable-based dyes.

Mixed Sources
FSC

*This is for all Indigenous Peoples,
and for A.S. as always*

Contents

~~~~~~~~~~~~~~~~~~~~~~~~~~~~~~

A Note on Terminology

In my work, I use the term "Indigenous Peoples" almost exclusively, for two reasons. First, I want to acknowledge Indigenous Peoples as being "Nations" (however challenging that may be to define in the current context of Canada), and I wish to avoid the use of terms (such as "Indian" and other terms created in response to that term) that could imply a general agreement with the political, cultural and legal approach taken regarding Canada's colonization. "Indigenous Peoples" is commonly used in other parts of the world but is not in widespread use in Canada. Here, the term "Aboriginal Peoples" is more common, partly as a result of Canada's legal recognition for "Aboriginal people" (that is, Métis, First Nation, Inuit peoples) in Canada's 1982 Constitution. When referring directly to a particular Indigenous Nation in Canada, I refer to that Nation or a community of that Nation by the name it calls itself (such as Piikani).

Second, I avoid (unless directly relevant to the point being made) use of terms that inappropriately reflect the status, role and legitimate place of Indigenous Peoples in Canada as the original, but also co-founding, peoples of Canada; and terms such as "Indian" or "Aboriginal" (which reflect racist or legally narrow perspectives). I use "Aboriginal" when referring narrowly to, for example, statistics or laws regarding the three legally recognized groups in Canada (Métis, First Nation, Inuit).

I use "European" to refer to that original influx of people who colonized and created Canada. I use "Canadians" for those people who reside in Canada or have Canadian citizenship today.

In Canada, First Nations communities are generally located on "reserves," whereas in the United States these are referred to as "reservations."

Finally, a note about "water." In 2008, the Chiefs of Ontario created a Water Declaration of the First Nations in Ontario. In that document they clarified that, to them, water includes "rain waters, waterfalls, rivers, streams, creeks, lakes, mountain springs, swamp springs, bedrock water veins, snow, oceans, icebergs and the seas." Certainly, this definition is inclusive of the generally accepted categories of groundwater and surface water (both salt and fresh) in all their states, and was probably intended to refer to all quantities of water, and whether they are of untouched, relatively pristine quality or have been degraded through use. My use of the term "water" includes all these states, locations, quantities and qualities of water.

Prologue: the Piikani, 2002

~~~~~~~~~~~~~~~~~~~~~~~~~~~~~~~~~~~

Most governments in Canada assert that
they own the water within their boundaries.
Given this, and with few exceptions, every use
of water in Canada requires a permit of one
kind or another from a provincial government.
Regarding waters that may be needed by First
Nations, however, there is complete uncertainty
as to who is in control of or responsible for or
can allocate that water. What entitlement do
First Nations have to water? Is it the same type
or scope of entitlement as other Canadians
have? If different, how and why and what
does this mean for First Nation and non-First
Nation water security? These are the questions
addressed in this book.

Almost all Indigenous Peoples disagree
with the notion of water ownership and that

provinces control this fundamental resource. A number of Indigenous Nations have taken to the courts to prove the existence of their unique Indigenous water rights and although the courts have not yet directly addressed the issue, the story of the Piikani gives a good indication of how extensive Indigenous water rights likely are and how these cases will be resolved.

The Piikani (or Peigan) Nation's traditional territories are located in southwestern Alberta around the confluence of the Oldman, Castle and Crowsnest rivers. Their reserve is about 12 kilometres below the Oldman River Dam, built by the Alberta government in 1986. The most controversial issue of the many that comprised this legal challenge was the Piikani assertion that their Nation possessed rights to the waters of the Oldman River. They based this argument on their interpretation of Treaty 7, which their ancestors had negotiated and which the Piikani continued to honour. In 2002, the governments of Alberta and Canada settled this long-standing water rights dispute.

The terms of the settlement should be seen as a dramatic harbinger regarding the strength of Indigenous Peoples' water rights claims and the scope of potential water conflicts in this country. Stuart Rush, one of the Piikani's lawyers, reported that the financial aspects of the settlement agreement included payments to the Piikani of $64.3-million into trust, with future additional trust income estimated at $125-million, annual payments of $800,000 (with increases to address inflation), $3,000 for each Piikani member, and $32.7-million for the settlement of claims against Canada for having wrongfully taken Piikani reserve land. The Piikani also received rights to participate in the Oldman River Dam Hydro Project.

Even with those large sums, the most significant elements of the settlement were those addressing access to water by the Piikani. The Piikani, federal and provincial governments agreed that the Piikani were assured water supply from the Oldman River to meet residential, community and agricultural needs. Regarding commercial development, the

3

Piikani acceded to the requirement that they receive a licence under Alberta law for 37,000 acre-feet of water per year for this purpose, thus forcing them to submit to Alberta's water-licensing regime, though only for this particular use.

The settlement contained a final, critical term: the Piikani stated, for the record, that they had no "prior or superior entitlement to water." Embedded in this requirement is the startling admission by the governments involved that the Piikani indeed possessed water rights; the sizable financial package and allocation of water to the Piikani indicated the expansiveness of those rights. It further acknowledged that the governments considered the water rights of the Piikani to be "first in line" rights, meaning these rights were first in priority, ahead of all other existing and future users of the Oldman River waters in Alberta.

Given the broad scope of the settlement, one might ask why the federal and provincial governments did not pursue the matter in court, particularly given the implications that can be drawn from the size and scope of the final agreement. The reason could be found in the nature of settlements themselves: no binding legal precedent was created. This is a very important consideration if one has a weak case and there is much at stake. Jack Glenn, who recorded the struggle to save the Oldman River in his book *Once upon an Oldman*, has suggested another reason. He argued that the federal and provincial governments were caught in an embarrassing dilemma regarding the Piikani water rights litigation:

> To deny the inference that Treaty 7 reserved some water for the Peigan is to admit that our ancestors swindled the Indians; to accept the inference is to admit that subsequent generations, including the present one, swindled the Indians by allocating all of the water to non-natives.

Lack of access to safe drinking water by First Nations has been symptomatic of a problem our governments refuse to address. The fair treatment of First Nations has never been consistently high on the priority list of governments in Canada; in numerous cases, such as fulfillment of treaty requirements, some governments have been outright obstructionist. To gain an understanding of Indigenous Peoples' water rights requires knowledge of the choices Europeans made (and Canadian governments continue to make) to minimize the important place of Indigenous Peoples in Canada. The impacts of these choices show up today as pervasive negative forces in the lives of First Nations, including whether they have access to fundamental requirements of a decent life, at the basis of which is access to safe drinking and household water.

It would serve us well to remember the case of the Piikani Nation and their water settlement as we consider who has decision-making power regarding Canada's increasingly threatened water resources, and who among the occupants of Canada is entitled to a fair share of this precious resource.

Some Inconvenient Water Truths

YOU CAN'T DRINK THE WATER THERE

If you lived in a country where one out of every six people you met lived in a town that had drinking water too polluted for human consumption, what country would you be in? "Indian" country.

As of June 30, 2009, the government of Canada reported 110 First Nation communities across Canada under a "drinking water advisory." Of those 110, the federal government indicated that 21 are "high risk" and require remedial plans because the problem is so severe.

In May 2008, in a review of six communities (chosen for their geographic and situational diversity), the Assembly of First Nations (AFN) and the Polaris Institute reported that they had found:

~ water tainted with uranium;
~ unacceptable levels of disease-causing
  bacteria;
~ tap water that is brown, has a foul smell
  and stains metal;
~ "disturbingly high rates of cancer and
  evidence of fish deformities."

The report stated: "There is no way that it would be accepted if people had to buy or be provided bottled water in other parts of the country for ten years. How can there be outrage over cases like North Battleford and Walkerton while few people know the extent of the long-standing crisis in First Nations?"

What is the impact of this water crisis? The HINI flu pandemic gives some indication. The Canadian Senate's Standing Committee on Aboriginal Peoples heard testimony in June 2009 that the impacts of the worldwide HINI pandemic were dramatically worse in northern Manitoba and Ontario First Nations, due in large measure to lack of running water, making it impossible for residents to observe recommended preventive health measures such as frequent handwashing. It has been reported that two-thirds of the more than 450 current cases of HINI flu in Manitoba are First Nations, even though only 20 per cent of Manitoba's population is Indigenous.

THE PROBLEM IS NOT NEW AND THE CAUSES OF IT ARE CLEAR

This problem of lack of access to potable water has been around for some time. Almost 15 per cent of drinking water advisories have been in place since 2002. In 2005, Canada's Office of the Auditor General charged its Commissioner of Environment & Sustainable Development (CESD) with reviewing the status of First Nation drinking water. The CESD reported that "despite the hundred of millions in federal funds invested, a significant proportion of drinking water systems in First Nations communities continue to deliver drinking water whose quality or safety is at risk." The CESD also noted: "When it comes to the safety of drinking water, residents of First Nations communities do not benefit from a level of protection comparable to that of people who live off reserves." Since 2003 when the federal government began its concerted effort to address First Nation drinking water issues, the situation has not dramatically improved. Of the 110 drinking water advisories that currently exist, 60 are dated within the last two years alone.

The CESD cited a long list of problems, including a lack of resources being spent to properly address needs. This despite $1.8-billion spent between 2003 and 2008 as part of the federal government's strategy to address First Nations drinking water needs. It is hard to imagine that, with the vast sums of money spent on this issue, there remains a lack of resources, but there does. Why?

1 MISREPRESENTATION OF THE AMOUNT OF MONEY TRANSFERRED

First, in 2004 the AFN estimated that, in general, of spending allocated to Aboriginal Peoples, only 67 per cent is actually transferred to First Nations; the remainder goes to other

Aboriginal groups, federal government admin-istration, and subcontracting of services to the federal government (to other levels of govern-ment and private-sector companies).

Second, water treatment plants are expen-sive to build and, more importantly, to operate and maintain. On average, a plant that services 600 people can cost over $6-million and require $150,000 per year to maintain and operate. Treatment plants are even more difficult and costly in northern locations, where weather and accessibility challenges are greater. This is also where most First Nations live.

The third reason relates to the relative level of resources that First Nations receive from the federal government. Every year, Ottawa transfers billions of dollars to the provinces to provide essential services. The provinces further disburse resources to municipalities. Given its jurisdiction over First Nations and their lands (under s. 91(24) of the *Constitution Act, 1867*), the federal government makes direct transfers of much the same nature to First Nations. But according to the AFN, the per capita funding the federal government gives to First Nation governments to provide services to their citizens is less than half of what is available to federal, provincial and municipal governments to provide services to the non-Indigenous population in Canada. The AFN indicates that the main reason for this lower funding is that federal government financial projections are based on, among other shortcomings, inaccurate criteria for determining population.

2 LACK OF A LEGAL FRAMEWORK

In addition to this relative underallocation of financial resources, the CESD also reported that the lack of a legal regime is a major cause of the poor state of First Nations drinking water. There are numerous reasons for this. First, governments do not overtly accept that First Nations have rights to water, which means that First Nations are not "allowed" to exercise an inherent jurisdiction to manage or use water.

Second, the *Indian Act* sets out the powers of Chief and Council on reserve, but it does not clearly provide for comprehensive powers related to water management.

Third, provincial laws do not generally apply on reserve. Therefore, whatever water protection laws exist neither govern nor benefit First Nations.

Fourth, there is no federal law that sets standards and rules that must be followed to ensure safe drinking water in Canada, including on First Nation reserve lands. In general, provinces have created a patchwork of standards and rules that apply within their boundaries (but not regarding First Nation lands and waters, as already noted).

This legal void regarding First Nation drinking water is known as "the regulatory gap."

REMEDYING THE PROBLEM WILL REQUIRE CEASING TO IGNORE IT

In 2006, largely in response to harsh criticism by the CESD, the federal government created an Expert Panel on Safe Drinking Water for First Nations to advise the government on how to address the crisis regarding the provision of safe drinking water for First Nations. The Expert Panel travelled across Canada and, after considering the advice of 130 presenters and the panel's lawyers, concluded that the management of First Nation drinking water required dramatic changes, including adequate resourcing and the creation of a binding legal regime that clearly outlined responsibilities and accountabilities. There is still no legal regime in place, although the federal government has recently shared some information with First Nations that it is in the process of developing a legal framework.

While the availability of water of drinkable quality isn't the only indicator of the health of a waterway, it certainly is an important one. Generally, if humans cannot drink the water there is a good chance the water will pose some significant risks for ecosystems that also depend upon it, especially if the low quality is a result of human-induced factors such as pollutant discharge from industrial operations or increased turbidity from deforestation-related sediment runoff.

Therefore, one solution to the drinking water crisis is to "go upstream," that is, to begin to address the drinking water problem by protecting the source of the drinking water. This was another important recommendation of the Expert Panel and was also considered by the inquiry into the Walkerton water crisis as a critical element of a multi-barrier approach to protecting drinking water sources. Source-water protection can be addressed through advance planning that takes into account both human and ecosystem needs.

This all seems straightforward enough, except that it has not been done. The issue of ensuring that an ecosystem has enough water to survive is, unbelievably, still highly contro-versial, especially in areas where people are facing serious water shortages that are affecting their lives and livelihoods. Where source-water protection planning is occurring, such as in Ontario, First Nations are not decision-makers, even though their waters – and by extension their communities – will be impacted by the choices others will make. This is the case almost

15

everywhere in Canada, even though more than 90 per cent of First Nation communities are located near or directly beside bodies of water and should have a significant decision-making role in what happens to those bodies of water. This exclusion is even more shocking when we consider (as we will in later chapters) that all Indigenous rights have, at their foundation, a connection to lands and waters. They all rely upon intact, functioning ecosystems.

We need to address this now because the world is quickly changing. Climate changes as a result of global warming are already dramatically affecting glaciers, which feed streams, rivers and lakes, and ultimately, through food production, us. We are losing the ability to accurately predict flood events, stream flows, ice cover and melt rates, precipitation rates and temperature changes. Yet demand for water is increasing and competition is already fierce. Oil sands development, mining, ranching, farming and hydro development all use enormous quantities of water and likely will continue to do so. Where do First Nations needs and rights fit among these myriad demands? This is the question we must answer. To understand the entitlements that Indigenous Peoples have to water, we must look back to our history and the choices that the three founding nations – French, English and Indigenous – made to create our country.

The History We Made

~~~~~~

A FOUNDATION WITH THREE HOLES IN IT

The Constitution of Canada is actually not a single document but rather a centuries-long series of documents. It created our country and sets out the foundation of our systems of government, as constitutions are supposed to do. But it also contains evidence of three dreadful decisions. A less cautious person than I might call them mistakes. Whatever you call them, these three historic decisions are critical to understand because they help to explain why addressing water problems in Canada, and in particular the water rights issues facing First Nations, is so very complicated and difficult.

In 1867, our country was created by the joining, through constitutional marriage, of the three provinces that existed at the time.

These were the Provinces of Canada (comprised of Upper Canada and Lower Canada, now called Ontario and Quebec), Nova Scotia and New Brunswick. New provinces have been added as the country has grown, while others from time to time question whether they would like to leave. It has been a rocky marriage occasionally and we have 58 constitutional documents building on our original 1867 Constitution to prove it.

We have witnessed our share of legal battles over the years as each level of government has tried to flex jurisdictional muscles and occupy space they think they have or should have. Defiant teenagers could learn a lot of strategy from these tactics. In our defence, we have only tried, as young countries must do, to interpret the rules the Constitution sets out. And there is only so much detail you can get down to when creating the founding documents of countries. They are documents that must live and grow by allowing governments to maintain a firm grip on the core values and principles of a country and its people with one hand while using the other to shake hands with new ideas, circumstances and people. This is how a country adapts when future becomes present.

Our Constitution is both typical and highly unusual as constitutions go. It sets out our system of government and explains who is responsible for what. It provides a list of powers, called the division of powers, that appoint responsibility to the federal and provincial governments to do the things we think are important for running a country. It sets out things like who can impose taxes (both federal and provincial governments), who runs the banking system (federal), who is in charge of regulating navigation (federal) and who can make rules regarding property (provincial). What is very important to know is that the Constitution, and in particular this list of powers, is the basic toolbox that governments and citizens use to regulate their actions according to the rule of law.

1 THE CONSTITUTION DOES NOT MENTION WATER

It is this very list of items in the division of powers sections, however, that is one of the most unusual things about our Constitution. It is just here that mistake number one was made: water does not make either the federal or provincial list – as anyone who works in the area of water *anything*, from management to policy to law, will tell you. A surprising oversight? Maybe. It could be that the people who wrote the Constitution were not hydrogeologists or engineers or anyone else who understood or cared that water could be taken, used and abused separately from the land it runs over, under or through. It could be that people at that time looked around at the vast quantities of water and ice everywhere in Canada and thought that it was not only impossible but absurd to even think of trying to figure out who could be responsible for such unlimited abundance. Who knows. But the lack of reference to water in the Constitution was instrumental in creating one of our most challenging ecological, human health and economic issues today: the mythical belief held by Canadians that we have, and always will have, vast amounts of fresh water available to us.

Without a specific responsibility for water, our use and abuse of water has gone largely unnoticed by Canadians content to look at the seemingly limitless lakes and rivers and translate this vista into a belief that water in our country is unlimited. Robert W. Sandford, chair of the United Nations Water for Life Decade of Action in Canada, reminds us that we in Canada possess only 6.5 per cent of the world's renewable freshwater resources, and that most of it (65 per cent) is not located where most Canadians live. The most respected scientists in Canada, including Dr. David Schindler of the University of Alberta, believe that as a result of overuse, poor management and increasing climate changes, we are in, or are nearing, a massive water crisis.

2 NEITHER DOES IT MENTION THE FIRST PEOPLES ...

The second regrettable decision was not including in the Constitution the recognition that the Indigenous Peoples were founding partners of Canada. For hundreds of years before our country was penned into existence, the

Original Peoples of this land were doing what Nations do: they were going about the business of providing for themselves, managing relationships with their neighbours and protecting their territories. After the arrival of newcomers to North America, they continued all these activities. However, diplomatic relations – everything from building and breaking alliances to formalizing relationships through oral and written agreements – took on increased importance, given the tendency of the newcomers to displace or destroy opposition and take land.

There are written treaties between Indigenous Nations and England or France that were signed hundreds of years before our Constitution was created. One of the more important ones is the Royal Proclamation of 1763, which first formally acknowledged Aboriginal title. This began a long line of treaties addressing many concerns and desires of Indigenous Nations and Europeans regarding relationships, land, settlement, governance and ways of life. These treaties made settlement possible and created the opportunity for the founding of a new country. Recognition of this pivotal role of Indigenous Peoples would have begun the country's governance on a foundation of respect between Nations and would have solidified Indigenous Peoples' role in Canada's ongoing governance.

3 ... EXCEPT IN ONE PLACE AND NOT IN A GOOD WAY

Despite this, Canada's first Constitution made no reference to anything regarding Indigenous Peoples, except in one place. This one reference is mistake number three. Astonishingly, the *Constitution Act, 1867*, in s. 91(24), sets out that the federal government has full and complete responsibility for "Indians and lands reserved for Indians." The inclusion of this statement was a pivotal and devastating moment in the history of Indigenous Nations. In a complete about-face, the federal government disavowed hundreds of years of history and turned its back on Indigenous Peoples. It adopted an assimilationist policy that was reversed only in the early 1970s and whose effects are still being felt to this day. Entire Indigenous Nations were essentially converted into federal property, in the sense that every aspect of their daily lives was now subject to scrutiny and required approval by the federal government.

When the Constitution drafters could have acknowledged the rich and critical contribution Indigenous Nations made to the creation of Canada, and affirmed Canada's commitment to seeing them remain strong and vibrant, the drafters instead placed them under the care and supervision of those who had every interest in ensuring that they ceased to exist. To say that this was immoral and unethical is to understate and simplify the matter greatly. Addressing the consequences of this act, along with the mindset that motivated it, has been a continuing battle that is fought daily by First Nations all across the country.

THE HISTORICAL RESULT: POLICY VACUUM
FOR WATER AND FOR INDIGENOUS RIGHTS

So what difference does all this make to water in Canada? First, we have created a legacy where water has no home address in our federal government. Only one of our provincial governments, Manitoba, has an entire department with full responsibility for water. In every other province there is no single place where responsibility rests. And for First Nation lands, there is no legislated responsibility at all.

In the best of worlds, this could mean a diverse approach where everyone treats water as if it were their responsibility. In such a world, everyone would choose to consider how every decision made might affect water, water sources and the use of water by all the forms of life that depend upon it. We would think in long-term ways about what is best in any given circumstance. But the opposite has occurred. The responsibility for ensuring the ongoing, Canada-wide quality and quantity of water to sustainably satisfy not only human but environmental needs has been forgotten. We have no national water policy, no enforceable national standards for drinking water quality, no binding national governmental statements about what we as Canadians consider to be the minimum water flows needed by all ecosystems. We have a system rife with gaps.

Second, we have a culture of opposition to Indigenous Peoples where, in large part, they are treated as a group whose problems and demands are unreasonable, bothersome and unending. There is an ongoing exclusion of First Nation governments from key discussions that affect the very future of our country. They are certainly not within the inner circle of decision-making regarding water resources in Canada.

But why should they be included? Individual Canadians do not have a right to sit at the decision-making table with governments. Should Indigenous Nations have a greater say in decisions than individual Canadians have? An answer lies in the fact that in 1982, after 115 years of denial, we Canadians decided to afford the highest level of protection to the rights of Indigenous Peoples. We did so by acknowledging and affirming, in s. 35 of the *Constitution Act, 1982*, the existence of the "aboriginal and treaty rights" of the Inuit, Indian and Métis peoples of Canada. These unique rights are based on the reality of Indigenous Peoples' existence on these lands as self-governing Nations when (or in the case of Métis, shortly after) Europeans arrived in Canada.

Hundreds of years after the fact, we may sometimes forget that Indigenous Peoples remain culturally and historically different from other Canadians, but also legally different. Our decision to recognize and affirm Indigenous Peoples' rights was one of the first and best actions of a legally new country (which is what we became in 1982 when, along with the Aboriginal and treaty rights clause, we decided to sever our long-standing constitutional connection with England). Canadians should beam with pride. With this decision, Indigenous Nations' legal status became unique in the world. More importantly, it opened the door to a reconciliation of the past based upon respect, dignity and honour. It meant that Indigenous Peoples have the right to a seat at the table.

This recognition is also important because with it comes the highest level of protection a country can give to rights held by a citizen, higher than any other law which that country has. Constitutional protection means governments have limits; they cannot run roughshod over Indigenous Peoples' rights. Much Aboriginal rights law since 1982 has been focused upon defining these limits to governmental power.

Notwithstanding this genuine progress, however, Indigenous Peoples are nevertheless forced, still today, to engage in constant legal and political fights to have their unique status implemented. Unless and until they win each of these fights, the common result is that Indigenous Peoples with rights, dreams, interests and ambitions are not included in important decisions that might allow or prevent the realization of such cultural uniqueness. This is certainly the case regarding their water rights.

The Death of Denial

~~~~~~~~~~~~~~~~~~~~~~~~~~~~~~~~~~~~~~

ACKNOWLEDGING INDIGENOUS RIGHTS:
THE HISTORIC JURISPRUDENCE

The late 1960s saw increasingly intense political opposition to the assimilationist policies of Canadian governments. The Constitutional protection of Aboriginal rights in 1982 was mainly a result of the signals sent by the Supreme Court of Canada through the *Calder* case in 1973.

Frank Calder, then a provincial MLA, sued the government of British Columbia, asserting that his people, the Nisga'a, had never given up their rights to their lands in British Columbia. The government of British Columbia argued that all rights had been relinquished (or "ceded") many years earlier, well before the province of British Columbia was created.

The Supreme Court of Canada did not agree. Instead, the judges decided that Aboriginal title to land could exist, although they were split as to whether it actually did exist in British Columbia at that present time. However, with this decision began the sea change in Canadian opinion regarding the recognition of the distinctive rights of Indigenous Peoples. With this case, the Supreme Court of Canada sent a message to Canadians and their politicians that it was no longer going to accept the legal denial of First Nations through refusal to recognize their pre-existing rights.

Canadians must take the time to understand the critical importance of *Calder*. Before that time, governments in Canada had assumed that Indigenous Peoples had no unique rights of any kind, and in fact had considerably fewer rights than other Canadians. All rights they may have had to lands and waters or to govern themselves had been eliminated through colonization of the country, through the "fact of Canadian sovereignty." This was the government's policy at the time, as seen in the federal White Paper of 1969. Further, the legacy of s. 91(24) of the Constitution was that First Nations did not appear to have a legal basis upon which to look after themselves. The federal parliament had actually legislated limits on their ability to seek legal redress on their own. The *Calder* decision sent a completely different message, a message of hope for Indigenous Peoples. The slow process of change had begun.

In 1984, more than a decade after the *Calder* case, the Supreme Court of Canada explained another fundamental element in the relationship between the Crown (in this case, the federal government) and First Nations: the fiduciary relationship. This case, *Guerin v. The Queen*, dealt with the federal government's mishandling of Musqueam First Nation lands, in Vancouver, which the government had leased to third parties. Given the role the federal government has assumed regarding First Nations and their lands and waters, the court held that the government is in a fiduciary, trust-like relationship with Indigenous Peoples, meaning the government has special legal and political obligations to act in Indigenous Peoples' best interests and to refrain from adversarial behaviour. This is especially important given the broad discretion the federal government has given itself regarding the lives and territories of Indigenous Peoples.

It took almost another decade for the Supreme Court to have an opportunity to explain exactly how to demonstrate that Indigenous rights exist. The court did this in a series of decisions, the most famous of which are the *Sparrow* and *Van der Peet* cases, in 1990 and 1996 respectively. In these cases, the court confirmed that Indigenous rights exist and set out the test, or framework, showing how they can be proven.

The court also explained, through these and later decisions, that neither the federal nor provincial governments could unilaterally take away Indigenous rights. Democratic governments do not unilaterally, without discussion or any form of consent, take away rights of their citizens. We do not have nor do we want this in Canada. Here, the democratic limits we place on our governments, both federal and provincial, require that they consult with Indigenous Peoples and accommodate their "claims, rights and ambitions" if they wish to make a decision that might affect Indigenous Peoples' rights. These are the clear limits that the Supreme Court, relying on numerous legal philosophies taken from the ancient English law of equity, the common law, the Canadian Constitution and in some cases the laws of other countries, has placed upon our governments and by extension on each of us.

JUST WHAT ARE "INDIGENOUS RIGHTS" EXACTLY?

The justices of the Supreme Court of Canada decided to base their Aboriginal rights doctrine upon the idea of a demonstrated connection to land on the part of the Indigenous Peoples claiming the right. So what are Indigenous rights? It is a sorry truth, and a shameful one at that, but despite over 35 years of deliberation by many people from all sides of the issue, the answer still depends on whom you ask. According to the Supreme Court, "Aboriginal rights" are rights that flow from Indigenous Peoples' occupation of Canada before colonization. These rights include Aboriginal title to land and are now protected under Canada's Constitution.

Indigenous Peoples refer to their rights as those that originate from the fact of their own existence, as Nations, residing and governing throughout these territories. These are their "inherent rights." In discussions about treaties, some call these inherent rights "reserved rights," meaning they are rights that were reserved by the Indigenous Nations and never relinquished through treaty-making processes. In the Canadian legal system, these are all called "Aboriginal rights."

The difference is not just about terminology. There is a fine but important distinction between the two approaches. Canada considers these rights as being valid once they are acknowledged by a court or the government itself (for example, through agreement). Indigenous Peoples, however, refer to their rights as being inherent in their Nations, given and limited by the Creator's laws and responsibilities, including the laws of stewardship and reciprocity with nature. These principles cannot be altered or narrowed by other humans, their governments or their laws, and this includes all Canadian governments. Neither can Indigenous Peoples themselves shed the responsibilities placed upon them by the Creator.

Canadians are correct to then ask, doesn't this conflict with Canadian sovereignty? The answer is, yes it could but it does not have to. The Supreme Court of Canada has tried to create a path through this dilemma by deciding that Aboriginal rights exist, with a framework for analysis to prove the rights, and by requiring governments to justify any impacts or limitations upon those rights. This latter element, called the infringement and justification analysis, must involve Indigenous Peoples themselves. It therefore provides the critical opportunity for accommodation of Indigenous Peoples' rights and concerns through negotiation. This process can, situation by situation, address inequities, achieve mutually acceptable goals, and, in the words of the justices themselves, "reconcile the fact of Canadian sovereignty with the claims, rights and ambitions" of Indigenous Peoples. Relatively recent cases such as *Haida*, *Taku River*, *Mikisew Cree* and *Dene Tha'* are examples of important decisions on this point.

WHAT ARE "TREATY RIGHTS"?

Another category of rights is that of "treaty rights." These can take two forms. The first are rights that pre-existed the negotiation of the treaty, and so the treaty merely recognizes these rights. Questions can be asked about whether the treaty modified the right somehow, but the source of the right remains clear: it is an inherent right that has merely been recognized in the treaty or in oral histories or written accounts of agreements made during treaty negotiations. Resource use rights (such as hunting and fishing rights) are of this nature, as are guaranteed entitlements to certain lands (treaty lands).

The second form of treaty right regards those new rights granted by another government (British, French or Canadian). These rights are generally set out in the treaty, but as with the first category, not always. Numerous commitments were made by governments as part of negotiations but were not documented in the treaties, and these too are legal treaty rights. These granted treaty rights include, for example, the right to receive certain annual per capita payments (however minute), equipment for farming, education assistance and medical care.

The progress of recognition regarding Indigenous Peoples' rights has been hard fought, case by case, situation by situation, for over 35 years. The negotiation of modern treaties, such as the one that recognized Nisga'a rights to govern more than 2,000 square kilometres of their traditional territories in northern British Columbia, was based upon the recognition of Nisga'a title to those lands. The federal government recognized the inherent right of self-government as an existing right under s. 35 of the *Constitution Act, 1982*. So did the Supreme Court of Canada, through cases addressing the scope of rights included in Aboriginal title, which the court has indicated includes "exclusive use and occupation of the land." Various courts have recognized rights to engage in a broad range of "practices, customs and traditions," including rights to hunt, fish, trap and gather and to engage in ceremonial, cultural and spiritual activities. Rights to trade have also been recognized. Courts continue to recognize new rights as they are presented with evidence from Indigenous Peoples. Indigenous peoples can exercise these rights throughout territories they traditionally occupied, not just on their reserve lands.

A SHAMEFUL FAILURE TO WALK THE TALK ON INDIGENOUS RIGHTS

But even where there has not been litigation proving that Indigenous Peoples' rights still exist in a specific area, the law now says we must give their claims the benefit of the doubt. There is good reason for this: without it, the only way to achieve peaceful resolution is through costly court challenges. Because of s. 91(24) of the *Constitution Act, 1867* and the government's fiduciary obligation, the Crown is supposed to watch over the rights and interests of Indigenous Peoples. Despite this, federal and provincial governments are still often the main opponent of First Nations and other Indigenous Peoples in court, asserting that they have few or no remaining rights.

The most recent example can be seen in Canada's rejection of the United Nations Declaration on the Rights of Indigenous Peoples in September 2007. This declaration, signed by 143 countries (with only four against), recognizes not only the inherent rights of Indigenous Peoples, including their right to self-determination, but also rights that flow from treaty agreements entered into with other Nations. It recognizes their rights to participate in decision-making in matters that might affect their rights and to decide what development occurs on their lands. The Declaration acknowledges that the recognition of the rights of Indigenous Peoples will enhance harmonious and co-operative relations between governments and Indigenous Peoples, based on principles of justice, democracy, respect for human rights, non-discrimination and good faith. The Declaration took over 20 years to negotiate. Canada refused to accept it.

It is a shameful display, and over the past few years, the Supreme Court of Canada has increasingly been sending signals that they have had just about enough of this kind of contradictory behaviour. The justices have been telling us all that Indigenous Peoples' rights lawfully exist, and that determining how to give effect to those rights is a matter that should be negotiated through fair and meaningful processes that address the real concerns of all people involved. Rights should not be determined through lengthy and expensive court battles. Despite this, the departments of justice at all levels of government appear to be concerned with minimizing the exposure of their respective governments to Indigenous rights obligations. Faced with this attitude,

Indigenous Peoples often, regrettably, have no other recourse. And as tensions over the sharing of water increase, the battles are not likely to end any time soon.

~~~~~~~~~~~~~~~~~~~~~~~~~~~~

WHAT IS A WATER RIGHT?

At the risk of oversimplification, when people speak of water rights, they are usually talking about the right to use the water, sometimes to the exclusion of other users. Expressed in those terms, a water right is akin to or is an ownership right. But it is difficult to classify it as such, and to do so conflicts with the nature of water (is this my molecule of water or yours, and where did it come from?). Water rights are really use rights.

There are at least four sources of Indigenous Rights to water. The first is supported by the argument that Indigenous Peoples had inherent rights to water before Canada and the provinces were created, and that these rights were never given up anywhere in Canada. Ardith Walkem and Nicole Schabus explain that these rights

> to, and in, water flow from the relationship of Indigenous Peoples to our traditional territories. Our right to water is an inherent right arising from our existence as Peoples and includes a right of self-determination with the power to make decisions, based upon our laws, customs, and traditional knowledge to sustain our waters, for all life and future generations.

These inherent rights require Indigenous Peoples to control or be involved as governments in decision-making regarding waters that are on their reserves, their treaty lands or their unceded traditional territories (such as in the East and West of Canada where there are no historic land cession treaties and Aboriginal title still exists; or anywhere else in Canada where treaties did not eliminate such rights).

However, almost all provincial governments, except Ontario and Prince Edward Island, assert through legislation that they own the property in and rights to the use of all water in their respective provinces, as a result of the lands being transferred to them when they were created as provinces (either through the *Constitution Act, 1867* for the three original provinces or, for the others, by subsequent legislation on the same terms and conditions as the original three). There are two important elements to these transfers (and the genesis of all provinces) that shed light on the existence of Indigenous Peoples' water rights.

First, it is presumed in general conversation about transfers of land that "land" includes "waters" that might be on, in or under that land. However, the law on this point evolved in fits and starts as Canada shifted from relying upon English law to the development of its own legal approach to governing water. There is a little-remembered debate that occurred on this issue between the federal government and Alberta, Saskatchewan and Manitoba. The debate took almost a decade to resolve; and it sheds some light on the thinking in Canada at the time and in particular seems to indicate we should be careful when making assumptions about rights to water.

When Manitoba was created in 1870, and Alberta and Saskatchewan in 1905, the federal government did not immediately transfer to them the lands and resources within their boundaries. The transfer finally occurred in 1930 through the Natural Resources Transfer Agreement for each province (these agreements being a source of contention for many Indigenous Peoples, as they were negotiated and signed without Indigenous Peoples' involvement or consent). However, for almost a decade afterward, records of parliamentary discussions indicate that the issue of whether water was transferred was hotly debated:

> doubts have been entertained on the part of the province whether the interest of the Crown in the waters and water powers within the Province ... was transferred to and vested in the Province under the terms of Natural Resources Transfer Agreements, the same not having been specifically

mentioned in the description of the natural
resources transferred to the Province ...

It was finally resolved eight years later to quiet provincial concerns. On June 24, 1938, the legislation that affirmed and gave effect to the three agreements was amended to "clarify" that federal water rights were indeed also transferred from the federal government to the governments of Alberta, Saskatchewan and Manitoba. The quote above is from that 1938 amending legislation.

DID FIRST NATIONS EVER CEDE ANY WATER RIGHTS?

What is important about this debate about provincial rights to water is that today's governments across Canada (if they say anything at all about the matter) assert that Indigenous Nations gave up all unique or separate rights to water at various points in the past. A common perspective provided by all provinces that are subject to land cession treaties with Indigenous Peoples is that water rights were given up when treaties addressing land were negotiated.

Yet the treaties say nothing about this. And unlike the debate over whether the Natural Resources Transfer Agreements included water, there has never been a clarification regarding this matter (although modern treaties, such as the Nisga'a Treaty, include negotiated water management responsibilities).

Added to this is the Supreme Court of Canada decision in *Sparrow* in 1990 that the only legal way in which governments in the past could limit the rights of Indigenous Peoples was through stating "a clear and plain intention" to do so. While there is legislation at both the federal and provincial levels by which governments give themselves the authority to manage and control water resources (such as legislation that purports to abolish riparian water rights), none state that their intent is to limit or eliminate Indigenous rights to water. In her review of the water rights possessed by Treaty 7 Indigenous Peoples in Alberta, Vivienne Beisel concludes that no government action to date (including the making of Treaty 7, the Natural Resources Transfer Agreements nor any other legislation) has extinguished any of the water rights of those Indigenous Peoples.

Given the importance of rights in our country, it is comforting that the courts require honourable behaviour by governments should they wish to alter or remove our rights. In 1938, the three new provinces demanded complete clarity to satisfy themselves that the federal government had in fact transferred all water rights to them. It is ironic and unfair, then, that these same governments insist that this level of clarity – in effect the same standard of behaviour – is not required when they regard Indigenous Peoples' rights to water. I believe that the Supreme Court of Canada, as the final arbiter of the behaviour of Canadian governments toward Indigenous Peoples in Canada, would not agree with this double standard. However, federal and provincial governments still have yet to prove (and it is their onus to do so) that First Nations peoples surrendered their water rights at any time in Canada's history.

Another element relates to the limits that were placed upon the transfers of land (and water), mines and minerals when provinces were created. The *Constitution Act, 1867* and the Natural Resources Transfer Agreements of 1930 state that the transfers of land (and water), mines and minerals to the provinces were *"subject to any trusts existing in respect thereof, and to any interest other than that of the Crown in the same."* Through this provision, the water rights and interests of Indigenous Peoples (having never been extinguished) appear to be guaranteed throughout the western provinces.

A second, related argument supporting the existence of Indigenous water rights is that all Indigenous rights include protections that are "necessarily incidental" to the exercise of the right. In the *Sundown* case (1999), the Supreme Court of Canada made an important decision that acknowledged that there are protected activities that accompany the exercise of Aboriginal and treaty rights. The circumstances of the case were that a First Nation man had cut down trees in a provincial park in Alberta and used them to construct a cabin in his hunting territory, which also happened to be in a provincial park. The court ruled that the man's actions were a "necessary incident" to the exercise of his treaty right. In another, earlier situation, in 1987, the Tsawout First Nation in British Columbia had been successful in permanently stopping construction of a marina in a bay that was the site of their traditional fishing grounds. In that case, *Saanichton Marina Ltd. v. Claxton*, treaty fishing rights were protected through protecting the associated water and seabed. It is a fine distinction, but it points to the willingness of the courts to link protection of rights to water to protection of specific water bodies. Despite this, the issue is far from settled as cases across Canada make their way through the legal system.

Based on this doctrine, all inherent rights and environment-related Aboriginal and treaty rights (including the right to self-government), likely include the right to use and determine the uses of water itself (as separate rights from those related to products of the water, such as fishing and harvesting rights). This would be an expansive list, and would include all aspects of water use and management with which we are familiar in our own lives, including domestic, recreation, navigation, industry, manufacturing, electricity generation, irrigation and flood control, among other uses. It is easy to see that it would be necessary to protect the quality and quantity of water in order to be able to implement a right to engage in fishing or harvesting from those water bodies. Right now, provinces tend to exercise these rights, and Canadians trust them to do so, but provinces do not manage them to ensure the maintenance of Indigenous Peoples' rights. That being so, there is a strong ethical argument, as well as a legal argument, that water management should be in the hands of those who have the most at stake in ensuring the ongoing protection of water.

DO RESERVES OF LAND INCLUDE THE RIGHT TO USE WATER? THE WINTERS DOCTRINE

The third argument supporting the existence of Indigenous water rights is that when reserves and treaty lands were created they included the right to use water. This argument is very important, and finds its origins in US law, where it has been definitively proven and implemented since the 1908 decision in *Winters v. United States* and subsequent cases. The *Winters* case involved a situation where, in a particularly dry year, upstream farmers diverted all the water from the Milk River in Montana, denying it to the downstream Assiniboine and Gros Ventre peoples of the Fort Belknap Indian Reservation. The farmers believed they had this right under Montana law, which, like western Canada, followed the "prior allocation" system of water rights. Generally, under this system, also known as the "first in line, first in right" system, a person acquired a right to use water by diverting it from its natural source and consistently putting it to a beneficial use. This is how settlers acquired water rights when the western lands of both countries were colonized. Proponents of this system see it as being certain and stable, while detractors feel it is unfair because rights holders are not required to share equally or equitably with their neighbours, even in times of shortage.

In the *Winters* case, however, the trial judge disagreed with the farmers' assertion of "first in line, first in right" and held instead that the Assiniboine and Gros Ventre peoples had prior water rights reserved through the treaty negotiated with the federal government in 1888 that created their reservation. This decision was affirmed all the way to the United States Supreme Court, and stands as valid law today.

There are six critical aspects of *Winters* that have direct relevance to Canada. First, the 1888 agreement that created the Fort Belknap Indian Reservation made no mention of water whatsoever. Despite this, the judge found that the agreement included an "implied reservation" of water rights in the Milk River by the parties to the agreement. This was necessary in order to accomplish the purposes of the Fort Belknap Indian Reservation, especially to irrigate the reservation lands.

Second, the judge held that the Assiniboine and Gros Ventre peoples were entitled to the quantity of water that was necessary, or might be in the future, for uses to satisfy the purposes of the reservation. This meant water to support all the beneficial uses of the lands and waters, whether for hunting, stock-grazing, agriculture or the "arts of civilization." For the Fort Belknap Indian Reservation, the allocation granted was almost the full allocation of water in the Milk River, regardless of downstream needs and even in times of aridity. Other cases have since held that water to satisfy fisheries preservation uses are also included.

The quantity of water that accompanies *Winters* doctrine water rights depends somewhat upon use, but has been related to the amount necessary to meet irrigation needs for the reservation's "practically irrigable acreage" or the amount necessary to "preserve the fisheries resource," that is, an in-stream flow right. For some reservations in the United States and reserves in Canada, this could mean large allotments of water indeed.

The third aspect of *Winters* that has relevance for Canada is that these rights exist even for waters that are not in or beside the reservation. The logic behind this is clear: it becomes even more important to ensure access to water when a reservation that does not have close or easy access to water.

Fourth, the logic inherent in the *Winters* doctrine should apply all across Canada (not just in the West, which uses the prior apportionment system), regardless of the water allocation system adopted by settler governments. Water is needed by Indigenous Peoples regardless of the mode of settlement chosen by Europeans. No cases have denied the application of the *Winters* doctrine to reservation lands located in states that operate according to riparian legal systems or those that use dual systems combining riparian and prior allotment. The application of this doctrine to groundwater remains legally unsettled, but given the connectedness of groundwater and surface water, logic should dictate a similar applicability of the *Winters* legal reasoning.

Fifth, the *Winters* rights to water appear to include rights to both quantity and quality of water (although the quality aspect has not yet received as much judicial attention as the quantity aspect has). This is common sense, given that domestic and municipal uses, irrigation for food production, animal stewardship and fisheries preservation require high levels of water quality.

Sixth, the *Winters* doctrine is not just a "special quirk of Indian law." It has been made clear over time that these water rights apply to all federal land reservations, whether they are for purposes of an Indigenous Peoples reserve or otherwise. This is treated with much hostility by state governments in the US, as federal rights do not depend upon prior appropriation (which is a state-level allocation system), and even if they did, they would be first in line. Further, federal uses for water are usually related to assuring protection of nature through ensuring adequate stream flows. Michael Blumm, a law professor who participated in the Northwest Water Law & Policy Project, describes the conflict in terms that have relevance to Canada and that make clear how Indigenous Peoples can get caught in the middle:

> The federal/state conflict over western water, largely between federal instream rights and states' diversionary [prior appropriation] rights, is one of the central conflicts in modern public land management and indeed over the future of the West. This conflict involves differences over whether public lands should be managed primarily for commodity production or for preservation. The conflict ... provokes deep-seated resentments that some westerners have for the federal government.

The *Winters* doctrine has not yet been directly relied upon in litigation in Canada, and because it is based on the US legal system, which is different from the Canadian one, an argument could be made that it is inapplicable in Canada's legal system. However, the doctrine appeared to play a deciding role in the Piikani negotiated settlement regarding their rights to water from the Oldman River. A number of claims are being asserted by Indigenous Peoples in both the Canadian East and the West for water rights, water ownership and rights to waterways, seabeds, lakebeds and shorelines that border their reserve lands and traditional territories. The logic behind the *Winters* doctrine should apply with as great a force in Canada as in the United States given that treaties and reserves were created in much the same fashion in both countries. In Canada, it was certainly the policy of the federal government at the time to limit the movements of Indigenous Peoples by having them become pastoral, and a number of Canadian treaties specifically mention agricultural pursuits.

ARE COURTS LOSING PATIENCE WITH GOVERNMENTAL FOOT-DRAGGING?

So what does all this mean for Canada? Optimistically, because the matter has not gone to the Supreme Court of Canada yet and we have a good indication of how such a decision might go, we have an opportunity to avert a water rights crisis. Although this book does not touch on it, there is an extensive body of water law in Canada, independent of

Indigenous rights to water. It is complex and varies widely across the country. However, given s. 35 of the *Constitution Act, 1982* and Aboriginal rights legal decisions, all Canadian water law is limited by the pre-existence of Indigenous Peoples' water rights, which is the main reason it is not addressed here. However, an important element of the needed water rights discussion will be how to balance sets of rights against one another. This will become an increasingly critical dialogue in times of water scarcity, when governments (federal, provincial and Indigenous) will have greater challenges making water choices that even come close to achieving a regional, economic, environmental, social and cultural balance.

Our history has shown that when it comes to Indigenous Canadians, our governments consistently avoid fulfilling not only basic protections that all Canadians deserve, such as access to safe drinking water, but also those special obligations that the law has placed upon them through the Constitution and court decisions, such as fiduciary duty and consultation responsibilities. Despite this, we must insist that this not occur again, and that Indigenous Peoples' water needs and water rights will be ensured.

In the *Winters* case, while one might have expected that the Assiniboine and Gros Ventre peoples took the farmers and state and federal governments to task regarding their water rights, it was the federal government that asserted, on behalf of the reservation and against the state, that the Native Americans had water rights that must be protected. This is surprising to me because of its stark contrast with the approach taken by governments in Canada. Here, the single greatest force of opposition to the recognition and implementation of Aboriginal and treaty rights has been federal and provincial governments.

The Supreme Court of Canada has been forced, as a result of rampant bad behaviour and neglect by governments in their trust responsibilities, to spell out the basic attributes of good governmental behaviour, by reminding the Crown that it always has a duty to engage with First Nations "in good faith"; that it is always bound by "the honour of the Crown," even when Aboriginal and treaty rights issues are not at stake; and that it must "avoid sharp dealing." The Supreme Court's frustration with federal and provincial governments' behaviour is increasingly apparent with each decision they make about Indigenous Peoples' rights.

Why are the judges so frustrated? Is it not their job to resolve disputes? Well, yes, of course it is. But they are also getting awfully tired of having to constantly remind us that we as fellow citizens should be working toward reconciliation of all our various interests instead of endlessly engaging in lengthy and expensive court battles, and for almost a decade now the judges have been repeating this same message. Of all the myriad resources Canada is privileged to have, this thinking is the most relevant and urgent regarding our underprotected, overallocated and increasingly precious water resources. It is well past the time when we should have begun to take the justices' message seriously. We must start now.

Limits to Rights

~~~~~~

THIS IS ALL SUCH ANCIENT HISTORY.
WHY SHOULD WE CARE NOW?

To many people, treaties and other forms of
protection or acknowledgement of the rights
of Indigenous Peoples seem like ancient or
irrelevant history. To some, these rights issues
seem endless; people think, and sometimes
ask, when is enough, enough? It is important
to remind ourselves that *everything* about our
lives today, not only those elements grounded
in law and politics, is based on ancient history. When a western province asserts that it
controls the water within its jurisdiction, it is
relying upon agreements reached between itself
and the federal government in 1930 and 1938;
and, just like treaties and Aboriginal rights,
both agreements are protected by law. When

we assert a provincial or federal government right to protect, use or destroy rivers, streams or lakes, we are ultimately relying on a long series of agreements that dates back almost 500 years. Those agreements reached throughout the centuries are our history, and were often hard fought for compromises to retain unity as a country. When it comes to engaging in the things we want to do today, we rely vociferously upon our rights to do so as originally set out in those documents.

Despite this, an important caveat exists in this discussion of rights. In our world, rights allow you to participate fully in the present and create your future. Respect for rights is the currency among races, genders, ages, societies and nations. I take it personally when governments do not live up to their end of the Aboriginal and treaty rights bargain, because, as a citizen of this country, Canada's history is my history. The choices each of us makes reflect on all of us. They are not "out there" in some government office or courtroom, or at least they shouldn't be. At the risk of sounding simple, for me as a

Canadian it comes down to this: I care about how we treat each other.

GETTING TO THE HEART OF THE MATTER OF RIGHTS

There are at least four problems at the core of the struggles of Indigenous Peoples to give meaning and impact to their rights. These can be seen in numerous Aboriginal rights cases, and they are the main barrier Indigenous Peoples face in fighting for water rights.

First, rights tend to be determined by those who already have them, and too often people who have them tend not to want to share them with others. This has certainly been the case regarding rights to water.

Second, if you are not human, rights are not of much use to you. In Canada, as in most countries of the world, humans are the proxy for everything else in the world, including nature. And humans are in a colossal conflict of interest. As Vine Deloria Jr., a Native American professor of history, law and political science, points out, the European scientific approach began with a separation of all things into human and non-human, with the latter category being synonymous with "thing, object and possession." Certainly, this also meant "lacking in soul or spirit." This separation can be seen not only in science but also in law, and has been basic in determining which entities get rights. Humans get rights, and that is that.

Third, while a right is an opportunity, freedom, entitlement, privilege, it also represents responsibility. However, rights tend to represent unstated or generally agreed-upon values of society and, as such, are only about those responsibilities the majority agrees with. So if you hold a different viewpoint, say, regarding your responsibility to protect or conserve nature, you will find you have little or no mechanism for implementing your responsibilities, especially when they bump up against the rights of the majority.

Fourth, there is no agreement regarding where rights come from. We all agree about the source of rights when they are written as laws and rules in constitutions, legislation, regulations and jurisprudence. Humans make these rights, and the source of the power to do so lies in the majority agreement of society. But what protections and recognition are afforded those rights or responsibilities that Indigenous Peoples believe are not granted, and thus cannot be changed, by humans?

Finally, the challenges facing protection of water resources today result from a system where rights holders cannot agree upon a course of action that is in both their own and the planet's long-term best interests. Regardless of who has which right, and to what end one wishes to use that right, all society must ask and answer whether we believe in limits to individual rights (regardless of who possesses them) to consume the earth beyond the point where we know we are damaging its long-term health.

A QUESTION OF CULTURE SHOCK

Because of this rights-based system, First Nations who work to implement water rights find themselves working simultaneously in two systems that are at odds with each other. The first system is the First Nation system of laws, which were conveyed through oral histories and which existed and governed First Nation societies long before settlers arrived. Elders, Indigenous scholars, traditional peoples and others in Indigenous Nations know, hold, share and teach these laws. The second is the current Western system of laws, which purports to give legal recognition to First Nation rights. The courts, in cases such as *Delgamuukw* and *Sparrow*, have agreed that both systems exist. The challenge lies in determining where and to what extent they exist. But the challenge actually begins before that, as a result of the differences in worldview and culture. This difference can make the exercise of Indigenous Rights very challenging. Here is an example.

When I first meet a First Nation person, if we want to get to know each other better or talk about anything else of significance, we often start the conversation by talking about where we are from, what lands or waters our families are connected to, or whom we might know in our respective families. The reason introductory discussions usually begin with explaining who you are and where you come from is that relationships to "place" and "other" put you into context; they give you validity, history and connection.

Indigenous people I know have taught that every Indigenous Nation has a unique culture, history and language that must be experienced to be learned. However, some elements are common to most. First Nations traditional spirituality starts from the premise that all elements of their birth, life and death are gifts from the Creator. The gift of existence comes with a sacred and immutable accord with the Creator, and so, first and foremost, First Nations legal and governance systems are built upon a spiritual foundation.

These gifts from the Creator come with significant responsibilities. All things on earth have spirit; almost everything is seen as animate and thus possessing soul. All things have standing on their own. The rocks are grandmothers and grandfathers, the earth is mother, the sky is father, and water is the blood that runs through the stream-veins of Mother Earth. The animus and interconnectedness of all things on earth are fundamental principles that require humans to engage in respectful relationships with all beings. Indigenous Peoples indicate that this stewardship responsibility is the primary characteristic of their relationship to the earth. It is the fundamental law from which other First Nation traditional laws flow. Winona LaDuke, in an address at Yale University in 1993, explained that

> Indigenous Peoples believe fundamentally in natural law and a state of balance. We believe that all societies and cultural practices must exist in accordance with natural law in order to be sustainable ... Indigenous People have taken great care to fashion their societies in accordance with natural law, which is the highest law. It is superior to the laws made by nations, states and municipalities. It is the law to which we are all accountable.

A fundamental principle of maintaining these respectful relations with the earth is reciprocity, which is about setting limits. It states that people must not take from the earth more than they need, and that something must be given in exchange as acknowledgement of the sacredness of that gift. For example, when an animal is hunted and killed, ceremonies are performed at the site before the animal is harvested, thanking the Creator and also thanking and honouring the animal because it made a choice and agreed to give up its life for human needs.

By contrast, European legal and governance traditions separate spirituality from law, people from the earth and its other inhabitants, and animate from inanimate.

This is not to say that all Indigenous or non-Indigenous Canadians subscribe to all of these beliefs, nor to imply that there is full agreement that the assumptions underlying these worldviews are correct and are held by all members of the respective societies. Further, a result of Canada's approach to colonization through assimilation of First Nations peoples is that traditional stewardship values that were respectful of nature and aware of limits are threatened. Just because a person, Indigenous or otherwise, has stewardship beliefs, this does not ensure that that person consistently lives by them. Vine Deloria Jr. worried that colonization may be ultimately successful through "the final absorption of the original inhabitants in the modern consumer society."

TOWARD SUSTAINABILITY THROUGH RECIPROCITY AND STEWARDSHIP

The relationships Indigenous Peoples have with their lands and waters today is even more complex than in the past. This is in large part because the Canadian government, through s. 91(24) of the Constitution and other repressive provisions, reserved to itself Indigenous Peoples' rights to choose how their traditional relationship with land and water would evolve, in particular, given exposure to European forms of economic development. It remains to be seen whether Indigenous

Peoples' traditional stewardship responsibilities will provide clear direction down a path to prosperity that is sustainable (in that it is governed, at first and last instance, by ecological limits) given the tremendous poverty, health and growth pressures that their communities face. If the direction is there, and they can follow it without the interference they have faced since the arrival of Europeans, they may achieve something the European-style economic development has not yet done: ecologically, socially and culturally, as well as economically, sustainable development that is respectful and protective of water and all beings that need and use it. So far, the jury is out.

~~~~~~~~~~~~~~~~~~~~~~~~~~~~~~~~~~~~~~~

**GETTING PAST "IT'S TOO COMPLICATED
TO SOLVE ANY TIME SOON"**

To move beyond the quagmire of blame and
inaction to a place of true forward motion on
water issues, we need to quit managing our
problems and start solving them. Author and
public intellectual John Ralston Saul believes
that most of the critical issues facing Canada,
such as poverty and health care, are capable
of immediate resolution. The barrier, he says
in *A Fair Country: Telling Truths About
Canada*, is the lack of will by a political elite
addicted to false complexity. This analysis
could also explain what feels like an ongoing
resistance to recognition of the legitimate
role of Indigenous Nations in Canada, and in

particular the lack of resolution of the water crisis facing First Nations.

Should we accept the imperative to move forward, the Royal Commission on Aboriginal Peoples (RCAP) has already provided direction to us, over a decade ago. Eloquently, they suggested four principles to form the basis of a renewed relationship with Indigenous Peoples: mutual recognition, mutual respect, sharing and mutual responsibility.

Following these principles, I suggest that the first step in solving the water crisis is that Canadians and their governments must accept that Indigenous Peoples have many rights, including water rights. Based on the broad spectrum of those rights, we can together begin to build a "relationship of renewal" that focuses upon reaching negotiated solutions to our water challenges.

GETTING WATER GOVERNANCE
REGIMES UP AND RUNNING

The first discussion that should occur is one about creating a legal and administrative regime, based on Indigenous Peoples' governance and water rights, to manage their water resources and solve the water-related problems in their territories. This certainly needs to include recognition of existing Indigenous laws that govern environmental use and protection, but may also involve the creation of new Indigenous laws addressing unique contemporary challenges. There is no reason why Indigenous Peoples' laws cannot form the basis of a system to govern their waters and work in partnership with other Canadian laws. Our Constitution, our courts, the Expert Panel on Safe Drinking Water for First Nations and the international legal system have all recognized it as a legal option. Remember as well that the federal and provincial governments of Canada have a long history of management of water (in the absence of complete jurisdictional clarity) through co-operative agreement. All it takes now is the decision to pull some extra chairs up to the table.

Our country also needs a Canada-wide water policy that includes regulated standards for all aspects of water use, including drinking water quality and ecosystem (in-stream flow) needs. In 1987, the federal government created a federal water policy (one that recognized "native" interests in water and committed to negotiations) but it lies dormant, mostly forgotten or ignored by those responsible for its implementation. Indigenous Peoples' involvement in the development and articulation of this national vision is critical to achieving the mutuality suggested by RCAP.

It is time to look seriously at articulating citizen-group rights to water, to ask ourselves, as both Indigenous and non-Indigenous Canadians, whether we are willing to come together to demand of ourselves and our governments that water be treated as a sacred element of our world that requires a higher standard of care, one commensurate with its unique status. Ralph Pentland, through the Polis Project on Ecological Governance, writes about the "public trust doctrine," and its desirability as a doctrine to unite us to safeguard water. This idea has great merit being based upon the idea of governments having a fiduciary duty to all Canadians to ensure that they sustain the essence of our water resources for all human and non-human life. This doctrine could be a legally, culturally and spiritually unifying concept for all Canadians.

ARTICULATING A NEW, CROSS-CULTURAL WATER ETHIC

Water, and its use by ecosystems, regardless of whether those ecosystems include humans, must be the subject of a sacred trust that requires citizens and governments alike to act in its best interests. The difficulty will, of course, be how we each might define "best interests." The sacredness and uniqueness of water puts it in a category all its own, one that is closest to the natural highest law, one above every other resource upon which life on earth depends. But we need to have a real discussion about this, one that leads to action which addresses the core issue of water's value to life. And all sides need to listen. As the Supreme Court of Canada stated in *Mikisew*, a meaningful discussion process "is not simply one of giving the Mikisew an opportunity to blow off steam before the Minister proceeds to do what she intended to do all along."

We can begin to work closely with Indigenous Peoples to articulate a new water ethic, one that combines the most long-term sustainable elements of the worldviews that created and today comprise Canada. This requires a "from source, to tap, back to source" approach, meaning it must address the full length and breadth of the needs for and use of water by Indigenous Peoples, all other Canadians and the environment itself. None of these three groups should be relegated to the status of second-class citizen. To do this means to immediately address the crisis facing drinking water and water for household use in First Nations communities, but also the 1,760 boil-water advisories across Canada reported by the Canadian Medical Association in April 2008. This statistic indicates a massive problem; the current approach is not working well and we need a new water ethic to govern our decisions.

Our water ethic should focus on prevention through source-water protection, protection of watersheds and alternative models of economic development that recognize the environmental limits and conservation approaches (such as the innovative work being done by Polis and Friends of the Earth on water "soft path"). We need honest discussions about the intensive use of water to create energy from oil and gas and hydroelectric development. We need to talk about water for agriculture and irrigation. Despite their benefits, these water uses come at a massive cost to waterways, ecosystems and Indigenous Peoples.

We should work together to define the value we place on water, and by that I do not mean economic value (although that may be one part of it). I mean value for life, for continuity, for genuine progress. Values are the unspoken elements that drive decisions, so we need to be clear about what we believe is best and why.

To care about our collective future, when we say "our" we must mean "everything": lands, waters, living and non-living beings. True reconciliation, the type that the Supreme Court of Canada repeatedly urges Canadians to work toward, will be achieved when we reframe our discussions and negotiations and base our choices and actions on what food activist Wayne Roberts, in *The No-Nonsense Guide to World Food*, calls the "balance" of "quantity with quality, consumption with engagement, mastery with humility, abundance with sustainability, comfort with challenge, mechanization with handiwork." To this I would add balancing law with spirit, past and present with future, forgiveness with accountability, and humans with nature.

Epilogue: the Navajo, 2009

~~~~~~~~~~~~~~~~~~~~~~~~~~~~~~~~~

The United States, the country of origin of the *Winters* doctrine, realized long ago that water should and must be shared with Native Americans, and that negotiated agreements are the only path to equitable resolution. On March 30, 2009, President Barack Obama gave final approval to omnibus legislation that gave full expression to the water rights of the Navajo Nation of Arizona, New Mexico and Utah. This law sets out water allocations to the Navajo Nation based on their *Winters* water rights. This settlement can help us see how important *Winters* rights are and thereby avoid protracted battles that waste the time, patience and ultimately the professional lives of those involved in the struggle. We can also see that the agreement reached is similar in scope to that of the Piikani in Alberta, and therefore both are likely fair and reasonable.

Under the Navajo-Gallup Water Supply Project, the Navajo Nation can use 27,000 acre-feet/year for municipal, industrial, commercial, domestic and stock-watering purposes. They can use this water to "generate hydroelectric development for the sole use and benefit" of the Navajo Nation. The Project was granted $870-million for its development. This money may be used to develop or restore the water supply project, but may also be used to restore fish or wildlife habitat or improve other environmental conditions within the river basin.

The agreement stipulates that the Navajo are entitled to develop groundwater wells to take 1,670 acre-feet/year of water from the San Juan River Basin, and 1,530 acre-feet/year from the Little Colorado and the Rio Grande River Basins. The development of wells in the San Juan River Basin receives an initial $30-million, with the other wells to be allocated funding as necessary over the next 15 years.

The agreement also quantifies Navajo irrigation-related water rights to divert large quantities of water: 508,000 acre-feet/year from the San Juan River for irrigation (through the existing Navajo Indian Irrigation Project), with a maximum depletion of 270,000 acre-feet/year (depletion is defined as diverted water minus return flows). This entitlement of water is the quantity needed to irrigate 110,630 acres of Navajo land. To understand the scope of this water entitlement, compare it to the Colorado River Compact (1922), which divides up the water allocations of the Colorado River among seven American states. For example, that agreement gives the entire states of Nevada and Arizona just 300,000 and 50,000 acre-feet per year respectively.

Irrigation uses include aquaculture and domestic, industrial or commercial purposes relating to agricultural production and processing. It also includes the use of the irrigation water to "generate hydroelectric development for the sole use and benefit" of the Navajo Nation. Additional amounts of over $34-million are allocated for other irrigation-related projects.

The agreement creates a water development trust fund of $50-million (built over ten years) that can be used by the Navajo Nation to address water project needs and water conservation. It also stipulates that the Navajo will not lose the agreed-upon rights to water through non-use. The Navajo affirm in this agreement that they are not giving up rights they have to sue regarding water-quality issues.

When considering the potential water and water rights claims of Canadian First Nations, it is also instructive to review what the Navajo agreed to release as part of this agreement (given that they can only release that which they possess). Among other things, they released all claims against the United States regarding:

> damages, losses, or injuries to water, water rights, land, or natural resources due to loss of water or water rights (including but not limited to damages, losses, or injuries to hunting, fishing, gathering, or cultural rights due to loss of water or water rights; claims relating to interference with, diversion, or

taking of water or water rights; or claims
relating to failure to protect, acquire, replace,
or develop water or water rights) ...

The Navajo and the United States governments chose a negotiated settlement based
upon recognition of Navajo water rights. We
could, and should, choose this approach.

Acknowledgements

Thank you to Peter Globensky, Dr. DeLloyd J. Guth, Irving Leblanc, Maurice Mierau, Anita Ozog and Robert Sandford for their valuable guidance and comments on the drafts.

Thank you to Don Gorman and RMB (Rocky Mountain Books) for their vision, willingness and support in seeing the importance of the water challenges facing Indigenous Peoples.

References and Related Reading

BOOKS

Bakker, Karen, ed. *Eau Canada: The Future of Canada's Water*. Vancouver: UBC Press, 2007.

Bartlett, Richard. *Aboriginal Water Rights in Canada: A Study of Aboriginal Title to Water and Indian Water Rights*. Calgary: Canadian Institute of Resources Law, 1986.

Beisel, Vivienne. *"Do not take them from myself and my children forever": Aboriginal Water Rights in Treaty 7 Territories and the Duty to Consult*. Saarbrücken: VDM Verlag Dr. Müller Aktiengesellschaft & Co. KG, 2008.

Deloria, Vine, Jr. *Red Earth, White Lies: Native Americans and the Myth of Scientific Fact*. New York: Scribner, 1995.

Dickason, Olive Patricia. *Canada's First Nations: A History of Founding Peoples from Earliest Times*. Toronto: McClelland & Stewart, 1992.

Funston, Bernard W., & Eugene Meehan. *Canadian Constitutional Documents Consolidated*. Scarborough, Ont.: Carswell, 1994.

Glenn, Jack. *Once Upon an Oldman: Special Interest Politics and the Oldman River.* Vancouver: UBC Press, 1999.

Herriot, Trevor. *Grass, Sky, Song.* New York: HarperCollins, 2009.

————. *River in a Dry Land.* Toronto: McClelland & Stewart, 2004.

Ignatieff, Michael. *The Rights Revolution.* Toronto: House of Anansi Press, 2007.

Jensen, Derrick. *What We Leave Behind.* New York: Seven Stories Press, 2009.

LaDuke, Winona. *All Our Relations: Native Struggles for Land and Life.* Cambridge, Mass.: South End Press, 1999.

Roberts, Wayne. *The No-Nonsense Guide to World Food.* Oxford: New Internationalist Publications, 2008.

Sandford, Robert William. *Water, Weather and the Mountain West.* Calgary: Rocky Mountain Books, 2007.

Saul, John Ralston. *A Fair Country: Telling Truths about Canada.* Toronto: Penguin Group, 2008.

Shurts, John. *Indian Reserved Water Rights.* Norman: University of Oklahoma Press, 2000.

REPORTS, ARTICLES, PRESENTATIONS

Assembly of First Nations. "Federal Government Funding to First Nations: The Facts, the Myths, and the Way Forward." Ottawa: Assembly of First Nations, 2004.

Blumm, Michael. "Reversing the Winters Doctrine? Denying Reserved Water Rights for Idaho Wilderness and Its Implications." 73 U. Colo. L. Rev. 173 (2002).

Canada, Office of the Auditor General. "Drinking Water in First Nations Communities." Chap. 5 in *Report of the Commissioner of Environment and Sustainable Development to the House of Commons*. Ottawa: Government of Canada, 2005.

Chiefs of Ontario. "Water Declaration of the First Nations in Ontario." Toronto and Thunder Bay: Chiefs of Ontario, 2008.

Eggertson, Laura. "Investigative Report: 1,766 boil water advisories now in place across Canada." *Canadian Medical Association Journal* 178, no. 10 (May 6, 2008): 1261.

Expert Panel on Safe Drinking Water for First Nations. "Report of the Expert Panel on Safe Drinking Water for First Nations." Ottawa: Government of Canada, 2006.

LaDuke, Winona. "Voices from White Earth Gaa-waabaabiganikaag." Presentation at 13th Annual E.F. Schumacher Lectures, Yale University, New Haven, Conn., October 1993.

McNeil, Kent. "The Jurisdiction of Inherent Right Aboriginal Governments." Vancouver: National Centre for First Nation Governance, October 2007.

Pentland, Ralph. "Public Trust Doctrine – Potential in Canadian Water and Environmental Management." Polis Discussion Paper 09–03. Victoria, BC: University of Victoria Polis Project on Ecological Governance, 2009.

Polaris Institute, with Assembly of First Nations & Canadian Labour Congress. "Boiling Point: Six community profiles of the water crisis facing First Nations within Canada." Ottawa: Polaris Institute, May 2008.

Royal Commission on Aboriginal Peoples. *Report of the Royal Commission on Aboriginal Peoples.* Ottawa: Government of Canada, 1996.

Royster, Judith. "A Primer on Indian Water Rights: More Questions than Answers." 30 Tulsa L.J. 61 (1994).

Rush, Stewart, QC. "Aboriginal Water Rights in Canada." Presentation to Just Add Water Conference, Saskatoon, October 3, 4, 2002.

United Nations. "United Nations Declaration on the Rights of Indigenous Peoples." A/61/L.67, September 2007.

Walkem, Ardith, and Nicole Schabus. "Indigenous Water Rights: Briefing Paper for Forum Participants." Presentation to Our Waters, Our Responsibility: Indigenous Water Rights Conference, Pinawa, Man., May 13–15, 2004.

CASES*

Calder et al. v. Attorney General of British Columbia, [1973] S.C.R. 313

Delgamuukw v. British Columbia, [1997] 3 S.C.R. 1010

Dene Tha' First Nation v. Minister of Environment et al., 2006 F.C. 1354

Guerin v. The Queen, [1984] 2 S.C.R. 335

Haida Nation v. British Columbia (Minister of Forests), [2004] 3 S.C.R. 511, 2004 SCC 73

Halfway River First Nation v. British Columbia (1999), 178 D.L.R. (4th) 666, [1999] 9 W.W.R. 645, [1999] 4 C.N.L.R. 1, 64 B.C.L.R. (3d) 206 (BCCA)

Mikisew Cree First Nation v. Canada (Minister of Canadian Heritage), [2005] SCC 69

R. v. Powley (2001), 53 O.R. (3d) 35, 196 D.L.R. (4th) 221, 152 C.C.C. (3d) 97, 40 C.R. (5th) 221, [2001] 2 C.N.L.R. 291, 80 C.R.R. (2d) 1, 141 O.A.C. 121 (Ont. CA)

R. v. Sparrow, [1990] 1 S.C.R. 1075

R. v. Sundown, [1999] 1 S.C.R. 393

R. v. Van der Peet, [1996] 2 S.C.R. 507

Saanichton Marina Ltd. v. Claxton (1987), 18 B.C.L.R. (2d) 217, [1988] 1 W.W.R. 540, 43 D.L.R. (4th) 481, [1987] 4 C.N.L.R. 48 (BCSC); affirmed [1989] 5 W.W.R. 82, [1989] 3 C.N.L.R. 46, 36 B.C.L.R. (2d) 79 (BCCA)

Simon v. R., [1985] 2 S.C.R. 387

Taku River Tlingit First Nation v. British Columbia (Project Assessment Director), [2004] 3 S.C.R. 550

Winters v. United States, 207 U.S. 564 (1908) 28 S.Ct. 207, 52 L.Ed 340

STATUTES*

Constitution Act, 1867, (U.K.), 30-31 Vict., c. 3

Constitution Act, 1930, (U.K.), 20-21 Geo. V, c. 26 [Natural Resources Transfer Agreements]

Constitution Act, 1982, being Sched. B to *Canada Act 1982*, (U.K.), 1982, c. 11

Omnibus Public Land Management Act, Pub.L. 111-11, s.10703(b), 123 Stat. 991 (2009) (U.S.)

*NB: Most principal Canadian cases and statutes are searchable in full text at www.canlii.org/en.